D1624165

To :-

From :-

OTHER BOOKS IN THE MINI SERIES:

To a very Special Daughter   Cat Quotations
To a very Special Friend   Golf Quotations
To a very Special Grandmother   Horse Quotations
To my very Special Love   Teddy Bear Quotations
To a very Special Mother   Book Lover's Quotations
Wishing You Happiness   Music Lover's Quotations

ILLUSTRATIONS JULIETTE CLARKE.
EDITED BY HELEN EXLEY.

Dedication: To Richard, in thanks for my happiness and peace and security, and in celebration of our twenty six incredibly beautiful years together.
    Helen

Published in Great Britain in 1991 by Exley Publications.
Published simultaneously in 1992 by Exley Publications in Great Britain
and Exley Giftbooks in the USA.

Reprinted 1992
Third printing 1992

Copyright © Helen Exley 1991

ISBN 1-85015-263-2

Acknowledgements: John Denver, "Annie's Song"; Reprinted by
permission of Cherry Lane Music Publishing Co.

Printed and bound in Hungary

Exley Publications Ltd, 16 Chalk Hill, Watford, Herts WD1 4BN, United Kingdom.
Exley Giftbooks, 359 East Main Street, Suite 3D, Mount Kisco, NY 10549, USA

What is our anniversary? Above all it is a celebration of a bonding, of a joining. Those years ago you and I said to the world: this is it. We are one. Henceforth we root for each other. We're a pair, a team. We declared ourselves to the world, and invited its approval. However nervous inside, however shaky and unsure of ourselves, henceforth we faced the world together. Thank God it was you. And thank God it's with you I celebrate today.

HELEN THOMSON

. . .

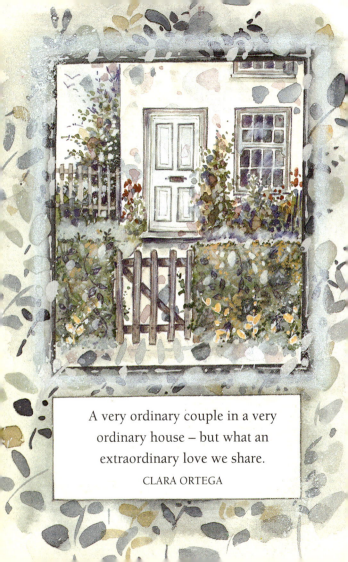

A very ordinary couple in a very ordinary house – but what an extraordinary love we share.

CLARA ORTEGA

ODYSSEUS TO NAUSICAA

May heaven grant you in all things your heart's
desire – husband, house and a happy peaceful home.
For there is nothing better in this world than that a
man and woman, sharing the same ideas, keep
house together. It discomforts their enemies and
makes the hearts of their friends glad – but they
themselves know more about it than anyone.

HOMER (8th century B.C.) from *"The Odyssey, Book IV"*

. . .

ALTHOUGH I CONQUER . . .

Although I conquer all the earth,

yet for me there is only one city.

In that city there is for me only one house;

And in that house, one room only;

And in that room, a bed.

And one woman sleeps there,

The shining joy and jewel of all my kingdom.

from the Sanskrit

. . .

FOR JONATHAN

Such love I cannot analyse;
It does not rest in lips or eyes,
Neither in kisses nor caress.
Partly, I know, it's gentleness

And understanding in one word
Or in brief letters. It's preserved
By trust and by respect and awe.
These are the words I'm feeling for.

Two people, yes, two lasting friends.
The giving comes, the taking ends.
There is no measure for such things.
For this all Nature slows and sings.

ELIZABETH JENNINGS, b. 1926

. . .

A GOOD WIFE

(She) is a man's best movable, a scion incorporate with his stock, bringing sweet fruit; one that to her husband is more than a friend, less than trouble; an equal with him in the yoke. Calamities and troubles she shares alike, nothing pleases her that doth not him. She is relative in all, and he without her but half himself. She is his absent hands, eyes, ears and mouth; his present and absent all . . . a husband without her is a misery to man's apparel: none but she hath an aged husband to whom she is both a staff and a chair.

SIR THOMAS OVERBURY (1581-1613) from *"Characters"*

. . .

The married state, with the affection suitable to it, is the completest image of heaven and hell we are capable of receiving in this life.

RICHARD STEELE

. . .

All married couples should learn the art of battle as they should learn the art of making love. Good battle is objective and honest – never vicious and cruel. Good battle is healthy and constructive and brings to a marriage the principle of equal partnership.

ANN LANDERS, b. 1918

LET'S NOT FORGET THE "FOR WORSE" DAYS . . .

. . . The lunch of rice hurled all over your
ungrateful man

. . . The huge door mirror smashed in a thousand
pieces in a spectacular and hurtful fight over a pair
of wandering eyes

. . . The fiery "I'm leaving right now" declarations,
and, worse, the slamming of the door, the keys
starting the car, and the actual leavings. The fears –
will she be safe? And the blind reaction – "I don't
give a damn." And then the merciful, heart-
wrenching, tearful return of the prodigal. "I love
you, I really do. And I'm sorry, terribly, terribly
sorry."

"Me too. Kiss me. Hold me."

Looking back, I suppose if we didn't care so much it
wouldn't have hurt so much.

I'm glad we cared. I'm even glad the fights hurt.

In retrospect.

M.C.G.

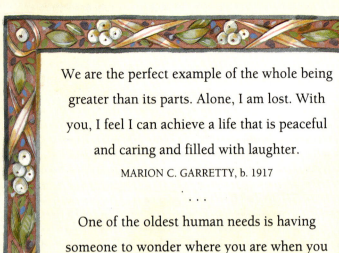

We are the perfect example of the whole being greater than its parts. Alone, I am lost. With you, I feel I can achieve a life that is peaceful and caring and filled with laughter.

MARION C. GARRETTY, b. 1917

. . .

One of the oldest human needs is having someone to wonder where you are when you don't come home at night.

MARGARET MEAD (1901-1978)

. . .

. . . love from one being to another can only be that two solitudes come nearer, recognize and protect and comfort each other.

HAN SUYIN (Mrs Elizabeth Comber), b. 1917

. . .

I know some good marriages – marriages
where both people are just trying to get
through their days by helping each other,
being good to each other.

ERICA JONG, b. 1942

. . .

Man and woman are two locked caskets, of
which each contains the key to the other.

ISAK DINESEN

. . .

Coupling doesn't always have to do with sex.
. . . Two people holding each other up like
flying buttresses. Two people depending on
each other against the world outside.
Sometimes it was just worth all the
disadvantages of marriage just to have that:
one friend in an indifferent world.

ERICA JONG, b. 1942

Campaigners against [marriage], from Shelley and the Mills on, have been remarkably crass in posing the simple dilemma, "either you want to stay together or you don't – if you do, you need not promise; if you don't, you ought to part." This ignores the chances of inner conflict, and the deep human need for a continuous central life that lasts through genuine, but passing, changes of mood. The need to be able to rely on other people is not some sort of shameful weakness; it is an aspect of the need to be true to oneself.

MARY MIDGLEY from *"Beast and Man"*

. . .

A successful marriage is not a gift; it is an achievement.

ANN LANDERS, b. 1918

In true marriage lies

Nor equal nor unequal. Each fulfils

Defect in each and always thought in thought

Purpose in purpose, will in will, they grow.

The single pure and perfect animal.

The two-celled heart beating with one full strike.

Life.

ALFRED, LORD TENNYSON
from *"The Princess – A Medley"*

. . .

There is no more lovely, friendly and charming

relationship, communion or company than

a good marriage.

MARTIN LUTHER

. . .

This bed is our island. Only the occasional cat shares our solitude. We listen to the voices of the sea, but pay no heed. We have shed the everyday. It sprawls forgotten on the chairs and floor. This is our place, our haven. Here we can rediscover one another, sleep in each other's arms. Here we can find ourselves again.

The world tears at us. Sometimes we scarcely know if we exist outside its rough demands. Only here, only in each other's arms, we rediscover joy. Only here we are ourselves, and so each other's.

PAM BROWN, b. 1928

. . .

What in the world is better than to wake up early and find the room aglow with first light, the streets silent, the air chill – and to turn to one another under the blankets, knowing it is Sunday Morning.

BRIAN E. WILLIAMS, b. 1961

. . .

Periwinkle

~ an ~
aphrodisiac

Heartsease

used in
love potions

Vervain

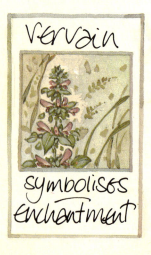

symbolises
enchantment

Herb Paris

powerful
~ in ~
love potions

ANNIE'S SONG

You fill up my senses like a night in a forest
Like the mountains in Springtime,
like a walk in the rain
Like a storm on the desert, like a sleepy blue ocean
You fill up my senses, come fill me again.

Come let me love you, let me give my life to you
Let me drown in your laughter,
let me die in your arms
Let me lay down beside you,
let me always be with you
Come let me love you, come love me again.

JOHN DENVER

. . .

It is as absurd to say that a man can't love one
woman all the time as it is to say that a violinist
needs several violins to play the same
piece of music.

HONORÉ DE BALZAC

. . .

Marriage is the beginning of an enterprise. In theory, two people have decided they love and trust and respect each other well enough to want to spend the rest of their lives together. They will build something that appears to outsiders something infinitely simple, but which, in fact, is infinitely complex – an ark to survive all weathers.

In reality, of course, people blunder into marriage for a dozen reasons – and often spend the rest of their lives on a disintegrating raft, held together with pieces of string. But any craft will stay afloat as long as its builders are happier to share its limitations than risk sharks. A boat can be merely a means of survival – or a means to a great discovery. Its course may be erratic, the repairs to its structure constant and haphazard – but if it is still afloat it has, with all its eccentricities, a jaunty air, a lived-in look, an air of comfortable companionship.

PAM BROWN, b. 1928

. . .

Do you take this man . . . this woman . . . to be your lawful wedded . . . from this day forth, to have and to hold, forsaking all others, for richer for poorer, in sickness and in health . . . till death us do part.

It's a pretty tall order. No employer would dare to demand such a contract. It's tantamount to slavery.

Pass me the papers. I'll renew my subscription.

RICHARD ALAN, b. 1936

. . .

What I thought was love was only a beginning. Every hour, every week, every year that I spend with you I discover a new dimension to loving.

PAM BROWN, b. 1928

You allowed me into your life. There has never been a greater gift. This last year has been a year of sharing our lives. Let's make this one just as special.

PATRICIA HITCHCOCK

. . .

Love seems the swiftest but it is the slowest of all growths. No man or woman really knows what perfect love is until they have been married a quarter of a century.

MARK TWAIN

. . .

How much the wife is dearer than the bride.

GEORGE, LORD LYTTLETON (1709-1773)

THOSE SPECIAL MOMENTS

Another year gone by.

So many memories. So many years.

Remember the places we've seen? If I say
Florence, Nairobi or Jamaica, other people
have mental images that travel in parallel. But
if I talk about Loch Hourne, La Berarde, Cwm
Nantcol or the Chess Valley, these conjure up
more private thoughts, our own special
moments. And it is the same with every
couple. The unforgettable shared days, the
personal things, the magic which only two
people know, are taken with them to the
grave. We have our own secret memory bank,
and a million thanks for the fact. Love you.

RICHARD EXLEY

. . .

People look at us and marvel. They don't know the secret of our quiet joy. We smile – for we don't know the secret either. It is an astounding gift we have been given.

MERCIA TWEEDALE, b. 1915

. . .

You can tell a good, surviving marriage by the expression in the partners' eyes – like those of sailors who have shared the battles against foul weather – and the scented airs of summer at sea. They welcome visitors – but are content with their own company.

MARION C. GARRETTY

. . .

No one knows our secret. We seem such an ordinary couple. How could they know the depth and wonder of our love?

BRIAN E. WILLIAMS, b. 1961

THANKS FOR THE MYRIAD LITTLE THINGS

. . . the smile across the crowded room

. . . the waking moment of finding you cradled,
snuggling, nestling amidst a pile of
bulldozed blankets

. . . the cups of tea brought without question in the
midst of hectic times

. . . the loyal and last-minute search for the passport
I should have got ready in the first place

. . . putting up with my cold feet

. . . managing to smile steadfastly when I crack the
same old jokes

. . . never telling I'm frightened to go to the dentist

. . . knowing when I feel small. About seven.

RICHARD ALAN, b. 1936

. . .

REASONS

Sweet one I love you
for your lovely shape,
for the art you make
in paint and bed and rhyme,
but most because we see
into each other's hearts,
there to read secrets
and to trust,
and cancel time.

TOM MCGRATH

. . .

Anthony and Cleopatra
Romeo and Juliet
Aucassin and Nicolette
Paulo and Francesca
Heolise and Abelard
Us.

PAM BROWN, b. 1928

. . .

It is wonderful to wake day after day, and to stretch out my hand and find that you are not a dream. And that you're always there for me.

HELEN THOMSON, b. 1943

. . .

The sum which two married people owe to one another defies calculation. It is an infinite debt which can only be discharged through all eternity.

GOETHE

. . .

In the arithmetic of love, one plus one equals everything, and two minus one equals nothing.

MIGNON MCLAUGHLIN

. . .

When we first met we were two people who loved each other. Now we are one person – two lives inextricably entwined and held by love.

PETER GRAY, b. 1928

. . .

Chains do not hold a marriage together. It is threads, hundreds of tiny threads which sew people together through the years. This is what makes a marriage last – more than passion or even sex!

SIMONE SIGNORET

. . .

See – this ring's so tight now that I can't slide it off. Let it be. The years have changed my hands but not my heart.

PAM BROWN, b. 1928

. . .